P9-CRW-089

BECKY SAUERBRUNN

Get in the game with your favorite athletes:

TAMBA HALI

Greenwood Public Library
310 S. Meridian St.
Greenwood, IN 46143

REAL SPORTS
CONTENT NETWORK PRESENTS

BECKY
SAUERBRUNN
David Seigerman

ALADDIN

NEW YORK LONDON TORONTO SYDNEY NEW DELHI

ALADDIN

An imprint of Simon & Schuster Children's Publishing Division

1230 Avenue of the Americas, New York, New York 10020

First Aladdin hardcover edition November 2017

Text copyright © 2017 by Real Content Media Group

Jacket photograph copyright © 2017 by Geoff Robins & Adam Pretty/Getty Images

Also available in an Aladdin paperback edition.

All rights reserved, including the right of reproduction in whole or in part in any form.

ALADDIN and related logo are registered trademarks of Simon & Schuster, Inc.

For information about special discounts for bulk purchases, please contact
Simon & Schuster Special Sales at 1-866-506-1949 or business@simonandschuster.com.

The Simon & Schuster Speakers Bureau can bring authors to your live event. For more
information or to book an event, contact the Simon & Schuster Speakers Bureau at
1-866-248-3049 or visit our website at www.simonspeakers.com.

Book designed by Greg Stadnyk

The text of this book was set in Caecilia.

Manufactured in the United States of America 1017 FFG

2 4 6 8 10 9 7 5 3 1

Library of Congress Cataloging-in-Publication Data

Names: Seigerman, David, author. Title: Becky Sauerbrunn / By David Seigerman.
Description: New York : Aladdin, 2017. | Series: Real Sports Content Network Presents |
Includes bibliographical references and index. | Audience: Age 8-12.
Identifiers: LCCN 2017002960 (print) | LCCN 2017012275 (eBook) |
ISBN 9781481482189 (eBook) | ISBN 9781481482172 (hc) | ISBN 9781481482165 (pbk)
Subjects: LCSH: Sauerbrunn, Becky, 1985—Juvenile literature. | Women soccer players—
United States—Biography—Juvenile literature. | Soccer players—United States—
Biography—Juvenile literature. | Women Olympic athletes—United States—Biography—
Juvenile literature. | BISAC: JUVENILE NONFICTION / Biography & Autobiography /
Sports & Recreation. | JUVENILE NONFICTION / Sports & Recreation / Basketball.
Classification: LCC GV942.7.S278 (eBook) | LCC GV942.7.S278 S45 2017 (print) |
DDC 796.334092 [B]—dc23
LC record available at https://lccn.loc.gov/2017002960

This story is for all the young girls and boys who appreciate that the third most important three-word phrase in the English language— after "I love you" and "Two scoops, please"—is **"Defense wins championships."**

CONTENTS

BECKY SAUERBRUNN: THE BASICS

BIRTHDAY: June 6, 1985

HOMETOWN: Olivette, Missouri (just outside St. Louis)

PRIMARY POSITION: Center back. Who better to describe what the position is all about than someone who plays it as well as anyone in the world? "First and foremost, your job is to not let the other team score," Becky has said. "You're the organizer in the back line, moving players in front of you into position, interrupting plays before they happen, or disrupting them as they happen. The position is evolving, becoming more of a quarterback role. Center backs, a lot of times, are starting the attack. They have the ball more of the time and are expected to move it forward and find the right pass. It's a good time to be a center back."

CURRENT TEAMS: US Women's National Team ([USWNT]; 2008, 2010–present), FC Kansas City (National Women's Soccer League [NWSL]; 2013–present)

FORMER PROFESSIONAL TEAMS: Boston Renegades (United Soccer Leagues [USL] W-League; 2005), Richmond Kickers Destiny (USL W-League; 2006–2007), Washington Freedom (Women's Professional Soccer; 2008–2010), Røa IL (Norway; 2009), magicJack (Women's Professional Soccer; 2001), D.C. United Women (USL W-League; 2012)

PREVIOUS US NATIONAL TEAMS: U-16, U-17, U-19, U-21, U-23

COLLEGE TEAM: University of Virginia (2003–2007)

SHORT LIST OF SOCCER ACHIEVEMENTS: *High school:* two-time National Soccer Coaches Association of America (NSCAA) Youth All-American; two-time *Parade* All-American; 2003 Gatorade Missouri Player of the Year. *College:* first three-time NSCAA All-American in the history of University of Virginia women's soccer; 2007 ACC Defensive Player of the Year; 2007 NSCAA Student Athlete of the Year. *Professional:* only three-time NWSL Defender of the Year (2013–2015); US Women's National Team: 2011 FIFA Women's World Cup (runner-up); 2012 Summer Olympics (gold); 2015 FIFA Women's World Cup (champion).

FIRST GOAL: Even back when she played with the Raiders, the grade-school boys' team in Olivette,

Becky tended to be defense-first. During one indoor tournament, the Raiders were "playing up"—going against teams one or two age groups ahead of them. And in one of those tournament games, the Raiders were getting annihilated. They were down big-time—by ten or twelve goals, as Becky recalls, which was about as lopsided a losing effort as she'd ever been involved in. At some point, Becky found herself deep in the offensive zone. Her teammate was bringing up the ball and decided to drill a pass across to Becky, who hadn't expected it (and might not have even seen it). "It hit off me and went in," she said. "I had never scored before." She remembers the boy who made the pass running over to her and lifting her up, and the rest of the team mobbing them. It was a nice celebration, but not one she would get to experience too often in her career. "From early on, I was a player who stopped goals. That makes me happy," Becky said. "The joy some people get from scoring goals is what I get from stopping someone from scoring."

FIRST GOAL FOR US WOMEN'S NATIONAL TEAM: As of this writing, we're still waiting. But she does have two career NWSL goals for FC Kansas City.

NICKNAME: "Broon," though the last syllable of her last name is pronounced "brunn" like "won," "fun," or hamburger "bun." In a video produced by the US Women's National Team, introducing members of the 2011 Women's World Cup roster to its fans, Ali Krieger mispronounced Becky's last name, calling her "Becky Sauer-BROON." It was pointed out—on camera—that Krieger had mistakenly used the more Germanic way of saying Sauerbrunn, which made sense. The 2011 Women's World Cup was being played in Germany, and Ali had been living there for the four years leading up to the tournament. She quickly corrected herself, but the damage was done. "Broon," Becky's new nickname, was born.

HER MANTRA: "Be ready." Just as Becky prides herself on being prepared for all opponents and game situations, she is conscientious about being ready for whenever an opportunity might present itself. "You never know who is watching or what opportunity is going to arise. When I look back on many moments of my career, if I hadn't been prepared, the next phase of my career never would have happened. Be ready for every possible opportunity."

WHAT YOU REALLY NEED TO KNOW ABOUT HER: "You can look at all sports—soccer, basketball, it doesn't matter. You would not find a better role model, a man or a woman, than Becky Sauerbrunn," said Steve Swanson, University of Virginia women's soccer head coach and an assistant coach on the US Women's National Team. "Who she is, what she represents, what's truly important to her, is all right there for everyone to see."

CHAPTER 1

FACING A CHALLENGE ... LITERALLY

Oh, man. That really hurt. Fifty-nine minutes into the first soccer game she ever played for the US Women's National Team, Becky Sauerbrunn realized something was wrong. She had just tried something she'd done on the soccer field a thousand times before: battling an opposing player for a ball in the air. Becky attempted to knock the ball upfield with a flick of her head. The forward from Canada's Women's National Team had other plans; she wanted to head the ball past Becky and in the direction of the Team USA net. It was a typical soccer moment in the middle of a typical soccer game.

Only this time, the Canadian player missed. Instead of striking the ball with her head, she accidentally headed Becky sharply and squarely in the middle of her face. And, man, did it ever hurt.

For perhaps the first time in her soccer career, Becky wasn't sure what to do next. She had never been hurt on a soccer field before, at least not to the point of having to leave a game. During her four seasons at the University of Virginia, she had missed a total of ten minutes of game time; she probably couldn't have given directions to the sidelines, she'd spent so little time there in college.

Should she take a knee, as players are coached to do from their earliest days, when they're learning to dribble a ball through a slalom course of mini orange cones spread out across a grassy patch in a neighborhood park? Should she try to get the referee's attention, to stop play long enough to get checked out? This whole situation was new to Becky, the pain and the uncertainty.

She did the one thing she surely knew how to do. She got up. Becky had decided she needed to shake it off, get back in position, and get ready for the next play.

After all, this was her first taste of a dream in the process of coming true: She was playing for her country at her sport's highest level. Years and years of practicing and playing, training and trying, working and waiting, had landed her here, inside the Foshan Sports Center Stadium in Foshan, China, at the 2008 Four Nations Tournament, starting on the back line of one of the best teams in the world of women's soccer. After everything it took to get here, she wasn't about to walk off the field, to leave her first cap—a player earns a "cap" every time he or she plays for his or her national team—while there was still time on the clock.

Becky had gotten opportunities to play before

because teammates had gotten injured. In fact, she was having the rare experience of starting her first game for the National Team because one of the team's other center backs had sprained her ankle in a training session in the days leading up to the tournament. No one gets to start their first cap. Was she really going to let a missed header knock her out of her National Team debut? And maybe make her lose the spot she'd worked so hard to get?

Then she reached up to feel her nose. And it wasn't exactly where it was supposed to be.

"My nose felt like it was on the wrong side of my face," Becky said later. "It was completely pushed in."

Becky hadn't noticed that her nose was bleeding, not until she looked down and saw blood flowing everywhere. Her first thought was that she should cup her hands and try to catch the blood. She didn't want to mess up her jersey—her brand-new USA jersey. Especially since she figured she'd be right back out on the field after the team doctors patched her up. No reason to leave a game over a bloody nose, right?

Wrong. Becky began to realize it was worse than some regular old nosebleed as soon as she saw the horrified reaction of her teammates. She recognized in their eyes the kind of look people get when they're watching a particularly gross or gory moment in a monster movie. Only they were looking at her face.

That was enough to send Becky to the sidelines for help. The team doctor took one look at her and immediately brought Becky into the locker room and laid out her choices: She could have it reset right then and there, endure one long bleed and be good to go, or she could go back to the hotel, calm down, and have it fixed later.

Before Becky was allowed to decide, the doctor told her to take a good look at herself in the mirror. That was all the convincing she needed.

"It was horrendous," Becky said. "I said, 'We absolutely need to do this right now.'"

That's what they did. The doctor laid her back, started feeling around her nose, noting all the cartilage that had been displaced. On the count of three, the doctor said, he would snap her nose back to where it belonged.

One . . . two . . .

"He did it on two. That's what doctors do," Becky said, recalling years later how with one quick move the doctor squished her nose back into place.

The team didn't have a protective face mask available for Becky to wear, so they fashioned one out of random equipment they could find in the kit—"MacGyver-inspired," Becky called it, remembering an old TV series from the 1980s about a secret agent who defuses bombs and saves the world by using whatever household items happen to be lying around at the moment. They fastened the mask to her face with Velcro from shin guard straps, and Becky was back on the back line.

Not for that game, of course, or the next one. But she was back in the lineup for the Four Nations final, which the United States won, 1–0, against China. The tournament-winning goal was scored by veteran midfielder Shannon Boxx. On a header. On an assist from her newest teammate. The one wearing the funny makeshift face mask.

In the years since, Becky Sauerbrunn has established herself as one of the premier defenders on the planet. She was honored as the Defensive Player of the Year in each of the first three seasons of the National Women's Soccer League's existence. She has earned more than a hundred caps for the US Women's National Team, winning an Olympic gold medal and a Women's World Cup for her country along the way. In 2016, she was named one of the cocaptains of the USWNT as the team prepared for the Brazil Summer Games.

Her playing style is defined by her smarts and

her toughness. "A silent assassin" is how National Team coach Jill Ellis once described her. Where did she first develop those traits that have been so vital to the success she has experienced on the soccer field?

Easy. Becky grew up with older brothers.

CHAPTER 2

OH, BROTHER

Grant and Adam Sauerbrunn needed a goalie.

It was the late 1980s or early 1990s, and roller hockey was gaining popularity in the suburbs that surrounded St. Louis, Missouri. Kids all across St. Louis County were lacing up their new Rollerblades and letting loose slap shots, either with hard plastic street-hockey balls or pucks (the ones with the buttonlike bumps designed to minimize friction and keep the pucks flying and gliding smoothly along the surface of a paved street).

The fever captured the Sauerbrunn brothers, as well as most of their friends in Olivette, a community about ten miles from St. Louis city proper. Roller hockey quickly caught on as the pickup game of choice, the sport all the kids would play together in the fading daylight after dinner until their parents called them indoors either to finish their homework or go to bed.

Scott Sauerbrunn, Becky's father, had grown up a couple of blocks away, and now he and his wife, Jane, were raising their kids in classic suburban style. The kids had everything they could have thought to ask for: big yards and a nearby park to play in, plenty of friends within walking distance, streets quiet enough for long chunks of roller-hockey action, uninterrupted by passing cars.

What they didn't always have was a willing goalie. So Grant and Adam got their little sister to be one.

Rebecca Elizabeth Sauerbrunn was born on June 6, 1985. By the time roller hockey was catching on, young Becky had already proven she was always game. She loved the times when her older brothers—Grant was about eight years older, Adam about four—included her in their games. They might be shooting baskets or throwing a baseball around the backyard, and they would ask Becky to chase down loose balls for them. That was a lot more fun than those times when the focus of their games shifted to something more along the lines of tormenting their baby sister.

"Sometimes, I was a plaything for them," Becky said. "They'd get bored and say, 'What do you want to do?' 'I don't know. Let's torture Becky for a while.'"

What Becky recalls as occasional "torture" her mother remembers more as "a fair share of brotherly mischief." (It should be noted that Jane Sauerbrunn is considered something of an expert on mischief, having spent thirty-three years teaching middle school, not too far up the road from Olivette in Ferguson, Missouri.)

Still, it sure felt like torture. Becky's brothers might, for instance, break into her room and kidnap one of the stuffed animals from her beloved menagerie of leopards, tigers, and cats of all stripes. Becky was cat-crazy in those days. When her brothers went into "mischief" mode, Becky would be ready to launch a full-on rescue mission. Many an afternoon was spent chasing down her brothers and retrieving her furry animal friends from wherever they had been imprisoned.

Later, Becky's brothers behaved more like the preteen boys they were at the time. Boys that age don't always want to play with their little sisters. For Becky, that was worse torture than the stuffed cat–nappings, and she didn't suffer those times graciously. Grant and Adam might, for example, be in the middle of a marathon game of Double Dragon on the family's Nintendo and Becky would want a turn.

"She'd come in, we wouldn't let her play, so she'd turn off the game," Adam said.

It's little wonder, then, that Becky jumped at the chance to play whenever her brothers asked. To play with them was far better than to be ignored by them. Even when playing with them meant playing goalie for their roller-hockey games.

However, there were a couple of problems when it came to playing goalie. First, Becky was only about five or six years old. She was so little, as Grant recalls, her Rollerblades could fit only three wheels down the middle of the skate. Standard blades for older kids always came with four.

The second and potentially more serious dilemma was that there wasn't goalie gear small enough to fit and protect the pint-size pip-squeak between the pipes.

Still, the siblings, like all creative kids, found a way to make it work. The boys improvised a set of goalie pads. (Turns out the Four Nations face mask from her National Team debut wasn't Becky's first exposure to MacGyver-inspired ingenuity.) They stuffed couch cushions into her shirt, slapped a catcher's mask over her head, and gave her a base-ball glove.

Then there was the pièce de résistance, the ulti-mate finishing touch: Becky's brothers took plywood planks and duct-taped them to her forearms. Years later, Grant insisted that the planks were taped to hockey gloves, not directly to Becky's arms. Still, she must have been quite the sight: a tiny, towheaded goalie with a puffed-out shirt, pink three-wheeled skates, and makeshift waffle-boards, fashioned from scrap wood and taped to her arms, flailing to fend off slap shots from fifteen feet away taken by the biggest kids on the block.

"She stood right in there and took a lot of pucks off the face," Grant recalled with more than a trace of admiration in his tone.

Essentially, that was the start of Becky Sauer-brunn's proud athletic career. Everything she achieved on the soccer stage—the All-America honors in college, the Olympic gold, the World Cup—can be traced back to those early years when she was a willing target in her brothers' street-hockey shooting gallery. But playing goalie wasn't all Becky had to endure.

When Grant and Adam got into tae kwon do, who do you think served as their dummy (with proper couch cushioning, of course)? When they wanted to test the laws of gravity, who do you think they launched into orbit off their couch, forever trying to see if they could toss her farther than the last time? It was fairly typical playful older brothers/willing little sister shenanigans, and occasionally the results were predictable.

Like the time the boys were playing baseball in the backyard and needed a catcher. No surprise, Becky—barely three years old then—was only too happy to oblige.

Memories of that event differ in the minds of the participants, as is to be expected after nearly thirty years have passed. Still, the basic facts of the case remain undisputed:

Grant was pitching.

Adam was batting.

Becky was playing catcher, probably a little closer to the batter than was safe.

Dad was mowing the front lawn.

It may have been on Adam's backswing or as he followed through after taking a full swing; no one is quite sure. At some point, though, the bat left Adam's hands, bounced, and smashed Becky in the face, splitting open her upper lip. As Grant put it many years later, "It exploded." [*Author's note:* Don't worry, not every chapter in this book features a facial calamity. I promise that this will be the last bloody episode in Becky's story.]

Becky, as you would expect, freaked out. The boys saw the blood, and they freaked out. Terrified of the unimaginable consequences of their parents finding out that they'd broken their baby sister's face, the brothers smuggled Becky inside and upstairs to a bathroom, where they found enough bandages to cover her bleeding mouth.

"Don't tell Mom and Dad," they pleaded with her, hoping perhaps that their parents would never notice that they'd practically mummified the bottom half of Becky's face. Becky made her way to the front lawn, where their father was mowing. Unfortunately for the boys, Dad noticed.

Scott took one look at Becky's bandaged mouth—wrapped so thoroughly she couldn't talk (part of the brothers' plan?)—and suspected right away that this was more serious than mere "brotherly mischief." He removed the bandage, saw that Becky's face was split from the bottom of her nose to the top of her upper lip, and decided a trip to the emergency room was in order. A plastic surgeon met them there, and Becky received her first six stitches.

"The boys got a talking-to after that one," Scott said.

As adults, neither brother will claim even partial credit for their sister's toughness, though clearly it was first honed at their hands. Is it any wonder that after a childhood spent being a crash-test dummy for her brothers' antics, Becky Sauerbrunn would be unfazed by anything she might face on a soccer field? Would suffer a broken and displaced nose and still not think about coming out of the game?

The best and most skilled scorers in the world can bring the ball deep into Team USA's zone, and yet Becky doesn't flinch. After you've survived a flurry of slap shots with only a plywood blocker pad and a couch cushion, there's not much you find too frightening to handle.

Actually, there was one thing in Becky's case. And her brothers played a big role in helping her overcome that, too.

CHAPTER 3

NERD SQUAD . . .
ASSEMBLE

Starting at center back for the US
National Team is something to be proud of, and
Becky Sauerbrunn certainly is. Not many soccer
players reach that level of success, men or women.
But Becky is also a proud participant of another
exclusive group.

She is a founding member of the US Women's
National Team's Nerd Squad.

It's not some secret society or squadron of
superheroes, though Becky once tweeted that "the
#USWNT Nerd Squad is kind of like the Avengers"

(and that she, obviously, would be Thor). Basically, the Nerd Squad is a group of teammates who like to make the most out of all the travel the National Team does to amazing places around the world. Rather than spending their days off and their downtime resting around the hotel, the Nerd Squad goes exploring. They go sightseeing, check out the local culture, try to experience what is unique and special about every place they visit. As Becky described during a 2015 interview on the television show *Men in Blazers*, all it takes to be a member of the Nerd Squad is "an interest in taking part in your surroundings."

Consider the team's trip to England for the 2012 Summer Olympics. On their first full day after arriving in London, several members of the American squad—Becky included, of course—took a side trip to somewhere particularly cool: They went to Hogwarts. Seriously. The group visited Alnwick Castle up in the county of Northumberland. It was built in the eleventh century and is home to the Duke of Northumberland and his family, but that wasn't the attraction. They went because it was one of a handful of castles used to represent Hogwarts in the Harry Potter movies (Harry's first flying lesson in *Harry Potter and the Sorcerer's Stone* took place right there on the grounds of Alnwick).

Becky's curiosity, her interest in taking part in her surroundings, can in many ways be traced back to a (near) lifelong love of reading. Wherever she travels, Becky goes with an open mind, and usually an open book—typically something you'd find on the shelves in the science fiction or fantasy section. She reads an hour or two every day that she can, especially during the most intense periods of National Team training camp.

She was into *Game of Thrones* before it was an HBO show. She is such a big fan of the Harry Potter series, she was tempted during the summer of 2011 to find a midnight screening of *The Deathly*

Hallows, Part 2 when the movie was released in Europe (unfortunately, she was pretty busy at the time—playing for the US in her first Women's World Cup, in Germany).

She loves *The Martian* by Andy Weir, *Ready Player One* and *Armada* by Ernest Cline, *Fates and Furies* and *The Monsters of Templeton* by Lauren Groff. According to her biography on the website for FC Kansas City, her NWSL team, her favorite book is *Ender's Game* by Orson Scott Card. She is always up for reading anything that will transport her to a richly described world—and temporarily away from the hard work she's putting in at soccer practice.

"Reading is my escape," Becky said.

That wasn't always the case.

When she started grade school, reading didn't click for Becky right away, which was a little odd considering her mother was a teacher and books literally lined the walls of the family home in Olivette (apparently, the Sauerbrunns boasted some well-stocked bookshelves). She enjoyed school and liked to learn, but she hadn't been bitten by the reading bug yet.

That's where Grant and Adam came in.

School nights in the Sauerbrunn household made for a scene familiar to many families: mom, just home from work, scrambling to get dinner ready; kids gathered around the dining room table doing homework. Often, the boys—when they weren't busy bundling Becky in blankets and propelling her off the couch—would help their sister as she struggled to make sense of the mysterious words on the page.

"They would be reading me a story and pause during a sentence, point to a word and ask me, 'What is that word?' If I didn't know it, they would act it out until I would get it. 'Oh, that's "rowing." I get it now,'" she said.

Soon enough, the light went on and a passion for reading was kindled. She read every Goosebumps book she could get her hands on and everything in the American Girl series, as well as all the different escapades of the Boxcar Children and the Baby-Sitters Club. That she would go on to major in English at the University of Virginia should have surprised no one.

Reading, though, would become more than a favorite leisure-time activity. Reading played an important role in Becky's development as a thoughtful, strategic soccer player—someone her club coach would one day describe as "playing chess while everyone else is playing checkers."

Back when Becky was beginning to learn the intricacies of playing a defensive position on the soccer field, a coach was trying to explain the importance of anticipating the play. There was an advantage to be gained by knowing what was going to happen before it happened. To improve as a defender, Becky was told, she needed to become better at reading the game.

She didn't quite understand what it meant to "read" a game. So she asked her mother, the teacher and avid reader, to explain it.

"As a defender, you're watching a story play out in front of you, just like in a book, where you have the plot and the characters and you can interpret what you expect their actions are going to be," Jane explained to her.

That made perfect sense to Becky. The better you know a character in a story, the easier it becomes to guess what he or she will do in a given situation. Same thing with a soccer player. If you know what her tendencies are—what she tends to do with the ball at certain times of the game or in particular parts of the field—you know what to expect. Then you can put yourself in position to stop her.

When Hall of Fame catcher Yogi Berra famously said, "Ninety percent of the game is half mental," this is what he was talking about.

"I get a feel for attackers, and sometimes I can

guess what they're going to do even before they know what they're going to do," Becky said. "I'm sure it's frustrating for them, but it's really enjoyable for me."

That ability to read a soccer game has served Becky like any other skill she's picked up and polished along her way to the National Team back line. She is credited with and celebrated for being a cerebral player—a player who thinks and plans rather than just reacts. In fact, one of the best examples of her game-reading powers came in one of the biggest games of her career.

An in-game injury to one of Team USA's starting center backs created an opportunity for Becky to take the field in the middle of the gold-medal game of the 2012 Summer Olympics. The American team had advanced to the final of the London Games by beating Canada in the semis, 4–3, and was now facing Japan. A year earlier, the United States and Japan had met in the final of the 2011

Women's World Cup. That game was tied 1–1 at the end of regulation and 2–2 after the overtime period expired. The World Cup came down to penalty kicks, which the Japanese won, 3–1.

Now the US Women's National Team and Japan were at it again, facing each other in the championship game, with eighty thousand fans in the stands at Wembley Stadium and the rest of the world watching on TV. And here came Becky Sauerbrunn, off the bench for the second straight game, into the midst of another winner-take-all showdown. Shortly after she entered the game, a turnover by the US created a two-on-one scoring chance for Japan. Two Japanese forwards were on the attack, with only Becky back between them and the US goalkeeper, Hope Solo.

Becky looked up and noticed something about the Japanese player advancing toward her with the ball: She had the ball on her left foot. Thanks to extensive time spent studying film of their opponents—getting prepared, learning those tendencies, *reading* the game—Becky recognized right away that this player was not a natural lefty. She was playing the ball on her weaker foot.

In a two-on-one situation, the lone defender has to make a decision, usually in the blink of an eye: *Do I cover the player with the ball and force her to pass? Or do I take away the passing lane and force that player to shoot?*

Becky read the play and knew exactly what to do: She angled her body, positioning herself between the player with the ball and her teammate. She decided the best move was to take away the option of a pass. The attacker would have to shoot the ball—with her weaker foot.

Sure enough, the player took the shot. Solo made the save. And the US went on to win the game and the gold by one goal, 2–1.

"After the game, Hope and I talked about that play," Becky recalled. "She said, 'You took away the pass, didn't you?' And I said, 'I knew you were going to make the save.' She made the save, we won the match."

Now that's what you call a good read.

CHAPTER 4

ONE OF THE BOYS

Jane Sauerbrunn remembers a day long ago when her daughter came home from elementary school with a question.

"Mom," Becky asked, "is it okay if I play with the boys during recess?"

"Sure," Jane reassured her. "What are the girls doing?"

"They sit and talk. The boys run around and kick a soccer ball."

Given the choice between gabbing with friends and getting in on a playground pickup soccer game,

Becky knew from a very young age where she wanted to be. When you're used to facing down slap shots from older brothers and their neighborhood buddies, the chance to play with boys your own age must be pretty appealing. It certainly was for Becky.

Becky's toughness may have sprung from growing up in that test kitchen of brotherly mischief, but the truth is, she also happened to be a pretty good little athlete from the beginning. She was a natural left-handed thrower, but her brothers were both right-handed. Which meant the hand-me-down baseball gloves were for righties. So Becky taught herself to throw and to bat right-handed. Just like her big brothers.

Her father, Scott, remembers there was an evaluation that would be administered to kids in Missouri when they were getting ready to enter kindergarten. The "test" consisted of the usual kindergarten assessments: The kids were asked to identify colors and demonstrate a working knowledge of their ABC's. And then there was the motor skills portion of the test.

Kids were asked to hop and to skip, not anything much more sophisticated or strenuous than that. Except that they were also asked to try to catch and throw a ball.

"The teacher would grab a ball and throw it to them," Scott recalled. "We were watching the boys and girls ahead of Becky, and the ball would bounce off their heads or they would hold their hands up and then watch the ball go right by."

Not Becky.

"Becky grabbed the ball and whipped it back to the teacher," Scott said. "With a chest pass."

So when Becky finally got to Old Bonhomme Elementary School, located across the street from Stacy Park and just a short walk from home, she gravitated toward the kids who played sports at recess. More often than not, at that age, that meant playing with the boys.

Soon, soccer with the boys extended beyond recess. From kindergarten into her late elementary-school years, Becky played on a community team with many of the boys from her class and her grade. They competed in the Olivette Athletic Association league, and the core of the teams would stay together through indoor and outdoor soccer seasons.

At some point, the team became known as the Raiders. The team uniform borrowed its logo from the Oakland Raiders, except the eye sockets were soccer balls. "Not exactly feminine," as Jane remembers.

Not that Becky minded. She loved being part of the team, and each season, as everyone grew and developed, she proved that she could hang with even the best of the boys.

Her teammates certainly didn't mind either. They respected her as a player and appreciated what she brought to the team. Once, a teammate named Cameron, the coach's son and the team's star forward, was lining up for the start of a game. A player on the other team looked at the Raiders defense he was about to match up against and mistook what he saw as an advantage.

"You've got a big problem," he told Cameron. "You've got a shorty back there and a girl."

Cameron glanced back to see what the opponent was talking about. He saw Becky, getting ready for the game to begin, and smiled.

"No, that's your problem."

Occasionally, there might be another girl or two on the team. Most of the time, though, Becky was the only girl on an otherwise all-boy team, but she never felt like an outsider. Her parents didn't mind, nor did any of the parents of the boys on the team.

Perhaps most important, she never felt singled out by her coaches. They treated her like one of the guys, going so far as to include her on trips to watch the Ambush, the Major Arena Soccer League franchise based in St. Louis for most of the 1990s. Sure, there was the one time her team won an indoor soccer tournament and, during the trophy ceremony, her coaches and teammates encouraged her to go stand up in front of everyone (a prospect she recalls as "positively frightening"). When she got her trophy, she understood why. Hers was unique among her teammates': the soccer-playing figurine atop the base on Becky's trophy was a girl. But that was about the only time her gender mattered. To anyone.

With her teammates' unwavering support, Becky was free to do what she loved most: play soccer. She became a fixture on defense for the Raiders, setting the stage for decades of soccer success to come.

A lot of women who grow up to enjoy careers as professional athletes have similar experiences. Many of them, at one time, played with and practiced against boys. Mia Hamm, one of the best players in the history of women's soccer, grew up playing with her brother. Many women's basketball teams at colleges practice against a squad of college men. ("It's not about a girl playing a guy," University of Connecticut women's basketball head coach Geno Auriemma told the *New York Times* back in 2004. "It's about two kids asserting themselves as basketball players.") Women in professional tennis often hit with male partners. Ronda Rousey, the one-time Ultimate Fighting Champion and gold medalist in judo, used to spar with (and beat up) men.

Becky always acknowledges that playing on the boys' teams gave her skills the time and opportunity to blossom. As she got older, though, she started to become aware that some of the boys were becoming stronger and faster than she was. Slowly, she realized that she needed to level the playing field. That was the first time she recognized the important role that soccer smarts would play in her development.

"I remember one of my teammates once saying to me, 'You're always where the ball is somehow.' He didn't say it in a mean way, almost more of an admiring way," Becky said. "Looking back, I think that's because I was starting to read the game. I didn't realize that's what I was doing at the time, but I was starting to figure out how to get myself into position."

Sometimes, Becky's approach to the game would result in a big play for her club team. Other times, it just meant being able to slide tackle and erase a scoring chance on the playground for the King of Recess. Wherever she played, it was clear: Becky Sauerbrunn could hang with whomever lined up across from her on the soccer field.

By the time she was nine or ten, it was also becoming clear—to Becky, her parents, and her coaches—that she would eventually need to find a new path forward. She was never one of the biggest girls in her grade to begin with, and the boys she competed with were getting bigger and stronger and faster and heavier. Also, being grade-school boys, they tended to be a little reckless, flying around the soccer field without fear of getting hurt or of accidentally hurting someone else.

It first occurred to Becky's parents during a game in which they saw two boys come together and kick at the ball at the same exact time. One of the boys wound up with a broken leg.

"That's when we started to hunt around for a girls' program," Jane said. "We knew we needed to make a change."

It's no overstatement to suggest that the change they made altered the course of Becky's life—and in some small way, women's soccer in America—forever.

CHAPTER 5

TENNIS, ANYONE?

For all the positive experiences Becky Sauerbrunn had in her many years playing on the Raiders team and with the various boys' teams in the Olivette Athletic Association, there was one moment that very nearly derailed her historic soccer career path before it ever really began.

Youth soccer teams often rotate their goalkeepers. They do it today, and they did it back when Becky was eight or nine years old and in the early stages of playing the sport competitively.

Once, during that time, Becky took her turn

in the rotation and found herself in net on a cold weekend day. The mere thought of being in goal—of potentially being responsible for allowing a goal and losing a game for her team—terrified Becky. Sure enough, on this particular day, one of the opposing players dribbled through the defense and got off a shot. The ball rolled between Becky's legs, resulting in a goal against her team, the first of her career.

Even worse, it was the game-winning goal. Or, from Becky's perspective, the game-losing goal.

For the brief drive home, Becky sat in silence, fuming over allowing a goal. Her parents pulled their green minivan into the garage and got out of the car, ready to go inside the house and go about the rest of their day.

Not Becky. She wouldn't budge.

"Aren't you coming?" they asked.

"No. I'm staying here."

"What's wrong?"

"I don't think I can play soccer anymore," Becky blurted out in a rush of anger and sadness and humiliation and guilt. "I can't be responsible for my team losing. I need to do something where I only have to be responsible for myself. I think I need to take up tennis."

Needless to say, the Sauerbrunns talked Becky off the ledge. She was back in uniform for her next soccer game (and, mercifully, not back in goal). The tennis career thing never took off.

Becky moved past that goal, but she never really got over it. That sickening feeling never left her. It still hasn't.

"I still carry it with me," she said, more than twenty years after allowing that game-losing goal through. "I feel responsible. That's why I never have been content with where I've been. There's always another level I can get to."

She is one of the best defenders on the planet, a vital contributor to teams that won both the

Olympic gold and the World Cup, and a cornerstone of her professional team. Yet somewhere in the back of Becky Sauerbrunn's mind, she is still that little girl who gave up the goal that beat her team. Most likely none of the boys who were on her team that day remember it. The kid who scored that goal almost certainly has no memory of it.

But Becky hasn't forgotten the feeling. She *can't* forget the feeling.

It's not the promise of glory that drives an athlete to greatness. Sometimes, it's the ghost of a long-ago goal that provides that one relentless reminder: There's always more work to be done.

CHAPTER 6

GIRL POWER

As far as birthday surprises go, this one probably wasn't as dramatic as, say, a fancy party or concert tickets or a really thoughtful gift (jewelry, maybe, or a puppy) might have been. But Tim Boul knew his wife, Jennifer, pretty well, and he knew she'd enjoy it. He never could have imagined just how well things would work out—for himself and for his wife, the birthday girl on this particular occasion. And for Becky Sauerbrunn, too.

Tim was on his way back home to St. Louis from Phoenix, where he had been coaching an Olympic development program (ODP) team from Missouri in a U-12 tournament (remember those initials *ODP*; they are an important part of Becky's story). On Tim's flight was a director from the J. B. Marine Soccer Club, where Tim had coached previously. They chatted about the tournament and about soccer in general. Inevitably, the conversation turned to Tim's future coaching plans.

Tim had taken a year off from coaching club soccer in order to coach a couple of teams in the Missouri ODP. He was coaching and traveling around the area as a referee, while Jennifer was working on finishing her master's degree. He had only just started to think about returning to the club level. As fate and good fortune would have it, here was an official from the J. B. Marine program dangling an interesting opportunity. Perfect timing, right?

By that point, J. B. Marine had already made quite a name for itself in soccer circles. The club was founded in 1978 by St. Louis businessman

George Foster, who was coaching his daughter's soccer team at the time and named her team for his business, Jefferson Barracks Marine Service Company. Foster's company cleaned and repaired barges that worked the Mississippi River. It was located nearby the Jefferson Barracks Memorial Arch Bridge, a pair of connected bridges that span the river on the south side of St. Louis. Most people didn't know that history. What they did know about J. B. Marine was that the St. Louis club program had become a soccer powerhouse in a short time.

Thirteen years into its existence, J. B. Marine claimed its first national championship: the 1991 U-19 girls title. By the start of the 2016 season, club teams from Missouri had won seven national championships across various divisions of girls' and women's soccer. J. B. Marine had won six of those seven titles. Missouri is the "Show-Me State," and no one in St. Louis put on a better soccer show than J. B. Marine.

Now, J. B. Marine wanted Tim Boul back. And Tim wanted to come back, though there was really only one age group he was interested in coaching: the U-14s. Turns out the U-14 job was the one the director had in mind for Tim all along. Amazing how life works out sometimes.

The U-13 team from J. B. Marine—the one that would become Tim's U-14 team the following season—was getting ready to play in a tournament, about two and a half hours away in Peoria, Illinois. Tim thought it would be a good chance to see what he was getting himself into. So he suggested to Jennifer—as her birthday surprise—that they go out of town for the weekend.

Which she thought sounded great.

To watch a soccer tournament.

"I should've expected that," Jennifer told her husband.

Tim came away from the weekend impressed with what he saw from J. B. Marine. It was a talented group of players. Several of the girls would wind up participating in the Missouri ODP.

One of those girls was a quiet, confident player who, until a couple of years earlier, had played pretty much exclusively on boys' soccer teams. Not many soccer fans would have noticed her, doing her thing as a defense-minded midfielder. Most fans tend to follow the ball and see the game only in terms of offensive skills: dribbling, passing, shooting, scoring. Bicycle kicks and fancy footwork are exciting. Marking an opponent, making sure he or she doesn't get the ball, not so much. Even tackling (basically, winning the ball away from an opponent) doesn't pack the punch it does in, say, football.

Offense makes *SportsCenter*. Defense is an acquired taste. In any sport, really.

Tim, though, observed the tournament through the eyes of a coach. A youth coach with experience in the ODP, a program that operates under one crystal-clear governing philosophy, according to its own website: "To identify players of the highest caliber on a continuing and consistent basis, which will lead to increased success for the US National Teams in the international arena."

Eyes like Tim's would notice the little things. Tim was fresh off an ODP tournament with U-12 players, so his eyes were tuned in to talent. He noticed Becky Sauerbrunn, though it wasn't because of any one thing she did out there on the field. It was because of everything she did.

"She didn't do anything exceptional," Tim recalled. "But I watched her play a number of games, and I noticed she didn't do anything wrong. She was always where she needed to be."

Exactly what her old Raiders teammates used to say.

Over the course of four or five games, Tim appreciated what he saw Becky doing: positioning herself with purpose, stepping into passing lanes, playing with her head up, moving the ball forward, distributing it to the best option, anticipating the play. You can't see from the stands when someone's out there on the soccer field thinking, but you can see the results of a play when someone was thinking about what she was doing.

She was a couple of years removed from playing boys' soccer, and Becky was beginning to distinguish herself among the girls her own age she played with and against. Not only was she reading the game. She was getting noticed for doing so—noticed by a coach who understood how special and important a skill that was.

"I quickly came to realize she was very cerebral about the game. She's always thinking two, three, four steps ahead, not just 'What should I do here?' but 'If I do this, what will the other player do?'" Tim said.

Once he began to coach the J. B. Marine U-14 squad, Tim—along with Jennifer, an accomplished college soccer player in her own right (maybe that tournament trip was the perfect birthday surprise after all)—saw evidence of Becky's serious approach all the time. It wasn't that she was shy or didn't enjoy her time with her teammates. She did. She would be right there in the mix, smiling and laughing and teasing with everyone else, whenever there was a water break during a practice or in the downtime when the coaches were setting up for the next drill. But when it was time to get back to work . . .

"When it was time to be focused, boom, she was right there," Tim said.

Most youth coaches quickly learn that full-squad scrimmages don't always make for the most effective practice sessions. When you have twenty-two players to teach and just one ball, 11-v-11 doesn't provide many opportunities to focus on specific aspects of the game. It's in the small-scale drills that the best work gets done—when attention could be paid to the details so vital to a player's

development. It was during those drills that Becky's soccer IQ was most apparent to her coaches.

Take the Up, Back, and Through drill. Many teams have used this familiar and fundamental two-on-one passing drill over the years, J. B. Marine included.

What happens in this attack drill is that one player—say, the center midfielder, which was Becky's position on that U-14 team—starts with the ball and plays a long pass ahead to a teammate in the middle of the field. Player 2 receives the pass, then lays off the ball back to the passer, who must run ahead to follow her pass. Player 1 regains the ball and dribbles for a moment to one side while player 2, who just laid the ball off, spins away from the defender at her back and bends around in the direction of the opposite goalpost. (It's sort of like a pick-and-roll in basketball.) Player 1 with the ball then feeds it through the defense, across the field, right to her teammate, who quickly blasts a shot

on net. (Can you picture what is happening on the field in this drill? The ball is passed *Up* from Player 1 to Player 2, who lays it off *Back* to Player 1, who then threads her pass *Through* the defense back to Player 2, who shoots and, ideally, scores.)

Lots of players can execute the physical responsibilities required in this drill: passing, laying off, shooting. Becky, though, was able to envision exactly how a play like this might unfold in the course of an actual game. In fact, she was even able to flip that play around in her mind and visualize what would happen if she were on defense and an opposing team tried to pull that very play against her team. Becky could picture herself as the center back, who might be tempted to chase the ball when it was laid off back to the first passer. That would be the wrong move. Instead, it's her job to drop back and cover Player B—the one rolling wide to get open for a pass and to take the shot.

It may be hard to picture this as you're reading.

For many players, it's challenging to understand what's happening even while practicing the drill. Not for Becky. Her physical skills were there. And those mental skills—her ability to connect the dots in her mind and understand not just how to execute the drill practice but how it might apply in game action—were starting to pay off.

CHAPTER 7

COMING UP SHORT

Before we continue the story of Becky Sauerbrunn's rise to the top of her profession, there is one thing you need to know. . . .

Becky isn't great at everything.

And she would be first in line to admit it. Not out of humility, though being humble is a cornerstone of who she genuinely is, as a person and as a player. Maybe it stems from her middle America upbringing. Maybe it's from being raised by parents who kept everything in perspective as their daughter climbed through the ranks of competitive soccer, from the local to the state level, then on to the regionals and nationals, and ultimately onto the world stage. Maybe it's because it's impossible to grow too big for your britches when you're flapping your arms around with plywood planks duct-taped to them.

Or maybe she's just wired that way. It's tough to be a me-first player and excel at playing defense. All positions on a soccer field require commitment, but defense involves sacrifice. You aren't going to score the game-winning goal or make the breath-taking play that's going to blow up YouTube. You aren't likely to wind up featured in the televised highlights (unless you're being burned for an opponent's goal). You aren't going to get your picture on the cover of *Sports Illustrated* like Carli Lloyd did in 2015 or on a cereal box like Mia Hamm in 1999. You give up the headlines and the spotlight and the stardom when it's your job to not give up goals. And you have to be perfectly fine with that.

And Becky is totally fine with that.

In fact, she'll earnestly tell you that she isn't great at any one element of the game. That aside from reading the game (let's be clear: That's the exact same skill that separated Peyton Manning from other quarterbacks), she has never found that one thing in her game that shines above everything else. She's never been the biggest or the fastest player on the field, the one with the niftiest moves or the hardest shot. Since she has never seen herself as spectacular at any one aspect of the game, she's spent her life training to be proficient at *all* aspects of the game. The classic jack-of-all-trades, master of none.

There's even one thing that was something that Becky wasn't even good at, let alone great.

"For the longest time, well after becoming a professional, I could not hit a long ball," she said. "I was terrible."

No joke.

Becky grew up on teams where long balls weren't a big point of emphasis. She played in systems that stressed keeping the ball on the ground, making short, accurate passes.

"That's one of the reasons I didn't get onto the National Team for a while. My game wasn't complete," Becky said.

Not only did she struggle to drive a pass long in a game, she struggled to do it in practice, too. In fact, long-ball drills were perhaps the only drills that Becky actually dreaded.

It wasn't until her coach at the University of Virginia, Steve Swanson, conducted a series of individual training sessions with her that Becky began to feel competent, if not entirely confident. Coach Swanson broke down every step of her mechanics, discussing with her the proper technique for every aspect of the long ball. He would stop her in mid-motion, examining everything from the placement of her plant foot to the way her strike foot grazed

Greenwood Public Library
310 S. Meridian St.
Greenwood, IN 46143

along the grass before making contact with the ball.

"When she came to Virginia as a freshman, she could not hit a long ball with either foot," Coach Swanson said, noting that her left foot was easier to develop than her right foot, because it hadn't developed as many bad habits as the right. "Becky deserves all the credit in the world. She went out and worked on it. She understood what she needed to do, changed the bad habits and developed the proper technique."

To this day, the long ball is not the strongest part of Becky's game. It's certainly not her favorite. But it's a good reminder that no matter where you are in your career, there is always work to be done.

Or as Becky puts it, "Anything that you can be trained to do can be improved upon."

Greenwood Public Library

CHAPTER 8

FROM ODP TO UVA TO USA

Remember those three letters we talked about earlier? *ODP?* The Olympic Development Program? That's where Becky's journey to the US Women's National Team really got going.

Let's make sure you understand how the ODP worked when Becky was going through it.

In soccer, as in many other sports, the level at which a club team competes usually is determined by age. A U-12 team, for example, consists of players under twelve years old (according to an established cutoff date); a U-18 is players younger than eighteen; and so on. When Tim Boul took over Becky's U-14 J. B. Marine team, everyone on the roster was younger than fourteen years old.

Each state has its own ODP, and although each runs things a little differently, the basic idea is the same: Players try out for their state's ODP. Tryouts tend to be open to the public, and anyone at any skill level is allowed to participate (as long as he or she meets the age requirements for his or her division). Many state tryouts are free—at least for the first day. In some states, only those players who are invited back for a second day have to pay.

At some point, the field of players trying out is cut down to a pool of about eighteen to twenty-four players. This becomes the state ODP team. When Becky made the cut, she was one of eighteen players who played for the Missouri team when it traveled to regional competition. The country is divided into four regions, and each region is made up of somewhere between twelve and fifteen state ODPs.

State teams come to the regionals and train with regional coaches, many of whom are college coaches, and all of whom were selected by the US Soccer Federation. They train together, and then the teams play each other: Missouri vs. Illinois one day, Missouri vs. Indiana the next.

All the while, coaches evaluate the top players in the region. They watch practices and games, talk to the state-level coaches and get their opinions of the best players in their own programs. At the end of these regional camps, the coaches select a regional team of thirty-six players. This is a pretty big deal in the US Soccer world.

Then the regional team goes to a national camp to train with and compete against the teams from the country's three other regions. There is a similar evaluation process and a similar selection process. And when it is all finished, a national team is selected in each of about half a dozen age groups.

If this sounds a little intense, well, that's

because it is. This is the time when soccer players—
and their parents—have to decide just how far they
want to try to take their game. It's challenging and
competitive, and these camps can be even more
emotionally demanding than they are physically.

"Physically, many of them can handle it," Tim
Boul said. "But can they accept the fact that, all of
a sudden, they might not be the best player on the
field anymore? Now they're up against kids from
all the different states coming together, the best
of the best. They could get hurt emotionally if they
don't make the team."

Becky was about fourteen years old when she
first played ODP at the state level. Her parents
weren't quite sure what to expect from the program; they just knew that their daughter was curi-
ous enough and dedicated enough to give it a shot.

"By the time she was in middle school, we knew
how committed she was to the sport, how much
time and energy she dedicated to it," Jane said.

And they knew how much she liked to compete.

"Even as a little kid, Becky always wanted to win," Jane said. "Some people say that you shouldn't keep score when kids are that little. It wouldn't have mattered. Becky always knew what the score was."

Some kids are content to be the big fish in their little local pond, and there's not a thing wrong with that. Some kids, though, want to see what else is out there, to measure themselves against the big fish from other ponds.

Some kids shrink from that sort of cutthroat competition. Becky blossomed.

She was placed into a group with players from across the state, most of whom were among the top players on their own hometown teams. Drill after drill, Becky showed she belonged with the best players the Show-Me State had to offer. She felt a familiar rush of confidence, the same awareness she once experienced with the boys on the Raiders: *I can hang.*

"What I found most enjoyable was the challenge of competing, comparing myself to everyone there and getting better," Becky said. "I was able to feel myself getting more and more comfortable and finding my way with this group."

Becky competed on the state level for a couple of years, each time with the goal of making the regional team. She never came out and told her J. B. Marine coaches what her ultimate goal might be. Maybe it wasn't yet clear even to her. But she did know there was a path ahead of her, and a sequence of steps she might have the opportunity to take. And if she didn't make the next step, she couldn't make the one that came after.

Even her parents didn't know whether Becky had a long-term plan. They just knew the process was a great growing-up experience for their daughter.

Once, Becky traveled with her team to an event in California. It was probably the first time she had been on a plane since she was very young. (Her brother Grant recalls a family ski vacation to Colorado: Little Becky wanted to follow her big brothers down the runs they were exploring. Sure enough, she picked up the brand-new sport quickly, and she spent the week snowplowing down the Rocky Mountains in her pink snowsuit, her brothers crisscrossing around her, keeping her safe.) Jane and Scott weren't worried about how Becky would handle the caliber of soccer competition she'd face out west. They were too busy wondering how she'd make her way through the airport in Los Angeles and find a phone to call a car from the ODP training center to come pick her up.

Becky grew up in the ODP, as a young woman and as a soccer player. When she was fifteen, Becky was competing at the U-16 level, and she went with the Missouri state team to the regional camp. The scrutiny there was tremendous, with the cream of the crop from each of twelve states hoping to rise to the top and make the thirty-six-person regional roster.

At the end of the pressure-packed weeklong camp, the coaches and regional directors held an assembly to announce which players they had selected for the regional team. Becky listened as they read the list.

She heard her name.

Rebecca Sauerbrunn, from Missouri, had made the Region II team.

They handed her an envelope, which was filled with paperwork that needed to be filled out before she could take the next step of her soccer journey. Becky clutched the envelope as she got onto the Missouri state team bus to head back home. She found a seat by herself, settled in, and sat there in silence for the longest time, clinging to that unopened envelope. For the first time in her life, the possibilities were beginning to register in her imagination.

"I was nervous to open it," Becky said. "I thought, 'This envelope holds my future.' It was the first time I wondered, how far could I take this? How far could I go?"

For starters, she'd go as far as Florida, where the four regional teams from across the country—North, South, East, West—met to train and practice, scrimmage and compete. Sure enough, when that camp was done, Becky had taken another new next step, claiming a coveted spot on the roster for the U-16 National Team.

It was also at that Florida camp that Becky first met Steve Swanson.

Steve had just left Stanford University to become the head coach of the women's soccer program at the University of Virginia. He'd coached the Stanford Cardinal to two Pac-10 Conference titles in his four seasons there. Before that, he had helped put the women's soccer program at Dartmouth on the map. At the same time he was taking over in

Charlottesville, he became the head coach of the U-16 National Team.

His first opportunity to work with Becky came at the U-16's first camp at the US Olympic Training Center in Chula Vista, California, a state-of-the-art training facility that today houses more than a dozen teams training for a variety of Summer Olympics sports. It has a forty-thousand-square-foot archery complex, six beach volleyball courts, and a BMX Supercross track modeled after the one used for the 2012 London Olympics. There are weight rooms and tennis courts and a track—and, of course, natural-grass fields for the US soccer programs.

Early in the very first game she played in that very first U-16 National Team camp, Becky gave up a goal. Well, as Coach Swanson remembers it, the goal wasn't Becky's fault. No goal is ever any one player's fault. She just happened to be the defender in closest proximity to the player who scored.

The goal isn't what made the greatest impression on the team's head coach. It was the way Becky responded to the goal that stuck with Steve Swanson. Rather than hang her head, lose her confidence, and fret that she had blown this rarest of opportunities, Becky responded to the challenge.

"She reacted the way you would want any competitor to react: *That is not gonna happen again. That's the last time you get something off me*," Steve said. "And she ate that kid up the rest of that camp. Even though she was faster than Becky and probably more athletic than Becky at that point in time, Becky shut her down."

Becky shut down attackers and opened plenty of eyes during that camp, Swanson's most of all. About the only one unimpressed by her performance was Becky herself.

At the end of the camp, Coach Swanson met with his players, asking each one how she felt about what she'd accomplished there. He had each player rate herself in comparison with the twenty-three other players on the team.

Becky put herself in the bottom three or four players.

Her coach didn't see it quite the same way. "For my perspective, she was in the top five."

Steve was struck by Becky's passion to improve as a player, something he saw right away. He's a big proponent of using video—shot at practice as well as during scrimmages and games—as a teaching tool, and Becky will never forget the first time Coach called her into his office to watch and evaluate films of her in action.

This wasn't exactly a collection of Becky Sauerbrunn's Greatest Hits. She was just learning to play on a four-person back line, and she found herself out of position more than she was accustomed to.

Needless to say, this film was not easy for Becky to watch. It was more lowlights than highlights, a series of clips that showed all the things she was not doing properly. She could feel her body curling into itself as she watched, almost as if it were trying to disappear from the room.

"He said to me, 'Becky, I know how good you can be, I know the potential you have. I believe you can reach the next level. I need to show you these things so you can learn from them,'" Becky said. "It was the most professional thing I had ever experienced. I remember leaving that meeting, thinking how I had this amazing coach who believed in me so much that he took the time to show me all these clips."

Coach Swanson remembers that session, too. And he remembers all the other conversations he had with Becky back then—in his office, on a bus, on the practice field, in the locker room, in an airport waiting area. He would spend as much time talking with a player as that player wanted. In Becky, he found someone who took an intense personal interest in her own development.

"I felt she could get extremely far, but it wasn't her talent alone that I was banking on," Steve said. "It was what she had inside, coupled with her talent. I wanted to help her reach her goals."

Not only was he instrumental in helping Becky reach her goals, he was right there with her as she achieved many of them. A few years after playing for him on the U-16s, Becky went on to play for him at Virginia, where she became one of the most accomplished players in the history of that legendary college program.

Then in 2014, he joined Jill Ellis's staff as an assistant coach on the US Women's National Team. He and Becky got to share many more moments together, including the celebration of winning the 2015 World Cup. That's quite a journey for a coach and player to take together.

CHAPTER 9

THE LONG RUN

After all their years together, Steve Swanson has no shortage of Becky Sauerbrunn stories to share. But there's one favorite anecdote that he feels captures the essence of what makes her special.

It happened back in Charlottesville, in the middle of Becky's college career, maybe during her junior season. Steve liked to find ways to challenge his players, and he had one exercise that would test them mentally and physically. They called it "Lap Ahead."

Basically, the team would line up together along

the perimeter of the practice field, adjacent to the University of Virginia's Klöckner Stadium. Coach Swanson and his players would prepare to run around the full field—which is 120 yards long, 75 yards wide (about one-fifth of a mile; like running around the outside of a regulation-size football field, plus an extra 50 yards or so). The catch was that Coach was considered to be a lap ahead. The players would have to circle the field once more than Steve did—to lap him. Once they gained back that lap, they had to catch him and tag him. Only then could they stop running.

It was not as easy as it sounds. Especially since Coach Swanson enjoyed toying with them. Sometimes he'd let them make up the lap, get close, just about within tagging distance, only to sprint away and out of their reach.

One day, when Becky was away, practicing with a national team, Coach put his team through the Lap Ahead challenge. Though she'd had the good fortune of being out of town and escaping the grueling test this one time, Becky wasn't interested in escaping.

"She came back and told me, 'I don't want to not do what the rest of the team did. I need you to do this with me.' I said, 'Sure, pick a day.'"

That Saturday morning, Becky and her coach went out to run Lap Ahead together. One-on-one.

Becky being Becky, she had done her homework. She had prepared. She discussed with her teammates what the proper strategy should be in this head-to-head challenge. The consensus was to come out running—to go as fast as she could from the get-go, gain as much ground as she could on that first lap, then keep pressing.

That was the plan. And Coach figured that would be her plan.

They ran ten laps before Becky could gain any ground on her coach. He wouldn't let her an inch in front of him, let alone a lap.

Over the next six or so laps, she started to catch

up to him and close in on that lap. He would let her get close enough to dive at him, only to pull away at the last second, leaving her first grasping at air, then gasping for air on the ground. Every time, though, Becky got up, and every time she raced back into striking position.

At some point, he let her lap him and tag him. The race was over. And it was clear who the winner was.

"If you had videotaped that session and watched it today, you would see everything you need to know about the internal makeup of Becky Sauerbrunn," Steve said. "She easily could have come back to campus and not worried about missing it. But she had to do what her teammates did. She couldn't miss anything. You would see how competitive she was. How much it mattered to her.

"She had that look in her eye."

Any striker who has advanced on the USWNT goal in recent years is all too familiar with that look.

CHAPTER *10*

THERE AND BACK AGAIN

As the press officer for the US Women's National Team, Aaron Heifetz has enjoyed the privilege of watching the best women's soccer players in the United States over the years. He's seen a lot of world-class soccer up close and personal.

Out of all that he's witnessed, all the spectacular moments and thrilling games, one play in the 2015 World Cup stands out among his favorites from the entire tournament. It didn't result in a goal or a sensational Hope Solo save. It was a play so seemingly routine, it likely wouldn't have warranted much comment from the broadcasters calling the semi-final game between Germany and the US And yet this soccer sequence is one he'll never forget.

It unfolded late in the scoreless first half. The ball was being brought down the right sideline by Célia Šašić, one of Germany's top forwards (Šašić scored a hat trick—three goals—in Germany's World Cup opening game and finished the tournament with six goals, earning her the coveted Golden Boot as the event's top goal scorer). Becky Sauerbrunn ran from her center back position over to cover the attacker, and she promptly took the ball away.

But that wasn't the end of the play.

Becky wound up with the ball in a tight spot—on the sideline, facing her own goal, with Šašić right on her back. One misstep here could turn into an attack situation for an elite goal-scorer. Many players, if not most, simply would have kicked the ball out of bounds and taken a moment for the defense to reset. Becky made a very different choice.

She wiggled away from the pressure, spinning away from Šašić and creating enough space to make a pinpoint pass to a teammate and get the play headed back in the right direction.

"Not only did she defuse the situation, she didn't give the ball up, and suddenly, here we are, going down the other way," Aaron said.

It was a moment he was sure went unnoticed by the masses, one he appreciates having witnessed and enjoyed, almost privately. Almost.

The masses might not have noticed. But Steve Swanson did.

On the US sidelines, the team's assistant coach watched Becky make just one more outstanding play for the National Team. It wasn't the kind of play that registers on a score sheet or draws cheers from the stands, but it was a perfectly executed play nonetheless. Even if it was a little risky.

When you watch Becky Sauerbrunn make plays like that, with such confidence and such consistency, it's easy to see why she's such a fixture on the US Women's National Team back line. In 2015, she played every minute of every game played by the US, including every minute of the FIFA Women's World Cup. She played every minute of the 2016 Summer Olympics. She's become so entrenched in the heart of the team's defense that it's really easy to forget that Becky's spot in the lineup—let alone on the roster—wasn't always so secure.

After all, she got her first call-up to the National Team in 2008 only because one of the defensive starters had been injured. Becky broke her nose in that first game, missed the next, but came back in time for the final. Still, after that Four Nations Tournament ended, so did Becky's time with the National Team.

The woman who wasn't inclined to leave the field even with a bloodied and broken nose now had to find a way to get back out there.

For many players, that could have been the end.

She had had her moment with the National Team, the highest-level team she could make. She had shown her talents and her toughness. She'd earned two caps for the United States, even picked up her first assist in the championship game.

Had Becky decided to walk away at that point, thinking she'd taken soccer as far as she could, no one would have faulted her.

Except, of course, the person looking back at her in the mirror.

Becky didn't quit. She accepted her coach's decision to send her back down to the U-23s, where she'd get back to working to improve her game. Fortunately, a new women's professional soccer league (named, appropriately, Women's Professional Soccer) was preparing to launch in 2009. The league held its first draft in the fall of 2008. With the third pick in the first round of the inaugural WPS General Draft, the Washington Freedom selected Becky Sauerbrunn. She joined a roster that already included three players from the National Team who had been assigned to the Freedom when the league was introduced: Abby Wambach (who has scored more goals in international competition than any player in history, men's and women's soccer included), Cat Whitehill (who played 134 games for the US Women's National Team), and Ali Krieger (Becky's once and future teammate on the National Team back line).

Becky played twenty games for the Freedom during that 2009 season; she even scored the first goal in franchise history. Then she promptly joined a professional team in Norway, spending a few months playing for Røa IL, a club based just outside of Oslo. Then she went back to the WPS and spent another season with the Freedom—anything she could do to keep playing, keep improving, and keep alive her dream of getting one more shot at the National Team.

Finally, in 2010, the call came.

Again, an injury created the need for Becky to

be called up to the National Team. She joined the squad during its training camp for the CONCACAF Women's World Cup Qualifying Tournament, the event that determined which teams would advance to the 2011 FIFA Women's World Cup. Becky wound up playing one match in the qualifying event and appearing in five games over the course of the 2010 season. Playing time was limited, but she remained undeterred. She was on the US roster. As it turned out, she was there to stay.

Becky may have been disappointed when she was released from the National Team in 2008, but she was never disheartened. She used those two years to work on her game, committed to becoming the kind of player no National Team coach would ever again be able to send down.

She knew that the National Team staff was coming to those WPS games, watching her and tracking her progress. Remember, her style is not one that is going to catch someone's eye in the stands or the press box. You have to be looking for her in order to notice the many ways she is affecting a game. As Tim Boul learned when he first watched her J. B. Marine team in that Peoria tournament, the more of Becky you see, the more impressed you are.

"I'm someone who grows on you over time," Becky said.

In 2011, Becky appeared in twelve games for the US Women's National Team. The one game she played in the World Cup that summer was the semifinal against France, when she stepped in to start in place Rachel Buehler (now Rachel Van Hollebeke), who had been suspended for a game after receiving a red card.

"Who does that?" Steve Swanson wondered years later. "To come into the semifinal of the World Cup, without having played in the entire tournament, and play that caliber of game? That was unbelievable in that kind of environment."

She took another step forward in 2012, playing in twenty-two games and making nine starts. Becky played only thirty-eight minutes in the London Olympics, but those were critical minutes. She came off the bench in the closing minutes of both the semifinal and championship games and helped the United States take home the gold medal.

Slowly, over several seasons, Becky grew into an indispensable player for the National Team. She evolved from someone who could hang with the best players at an ODP camp to someone who belonged with the best players in the world. She's grown from someone who made the team into someone who now makes the team go. She's gone from a replacement part to a key contributor to an impact player to co-captain of the world champion US Women's National Team.

In announcing her selection of Becky and Carli Lloyd as co-captains, head coach Jill Ellis described them as "two extremely professional players in both game and training environments" and noted that they both "embody the DNA of this program."

Like DNA itself, Becky's true contributions can be tough to map out clearly enough for the naked eye to appreciate. Minutes Played might not be the most glamorous of statistical categories—no fantasy soccer leagues factor that into their scoring systems—but those figures do tell a big part of Becky's story. You can't help your team if you're not out on the field. The fact that she is out there, for more minutes than practically any of her teammates, speaks to Becky's most important impact: Her teammates can always count on her to be there, to have their backs, and to make the steady, unspectacular, but absolutely essential plays that provide the foundation for winning teams.

"Becky will tell you that she's an ordinary person who has achieved extraordinary results," Coach Swanson said. "That has everything to do with the kind of person she is."

CHAPTER 11

ULTIMATE GOALS

There are a handful of moments in American sports history that will live forever.

Go ask your grandparents if they remember where they were when Bobby Thomson hit his "Shot Heard 'Round the World," the home run that lifted the New York Giants past the Brooklyn Dodgers and to the 1951 National League pennant.

Ask your parents what they were doing when Mike Eruzione scored his game-winning goal against the Russians in 1980, making everyone in America, hockey fan or not, believe in a Miracle on Ice.

Some moments are made of such magic and improbability that they can never be forgotten by anyone who witnessed them with their own eyes and ears and heart: Kirk Gibson's "I don't believe what I just saw" home run and his fist-pumping limp around the bases in the 1988 World Series. Christian Laettner's turnaround shot at the buzzer against Kentucky in 1992. Rocky still standing at the final bell in his first fight against Apollo Creed.

Okay, that last one is from a movie. It isn't real. But moments like these often seem like they were scripted by Hollywood screenwriters, like they were dipped in gooey drama and preserved in some perfect candy shell and frozen in time. They are the only true reality TV.

Becky Sauerbrunn has a moment like that. It was Saturday, July 10, 1999, and she was on the floor of her family room, back home in Olivette. Her father was in his usual spot—his rocking chair. Becky had recently turned fourteen, and her life that summer of 1999 was consumed with soccer, playing it and watching the US Women's National Team try to win the Women's World Cup at home on American soil.

The United States and China were at the Rose Bowl in Pasadena, California, facing off in the World Cup final. More than ninety thousand fans were in the stands, a crowd larger than had ever gathered to watch a women's sporting event in America. After regulation time, the teams had played to a scoreless draw.

The score remained 0–0 at the conclusion of extra time. The game and the World Cup would come down to penalty kicks.

Becky lay on the floor, her head in her hands, four feet from the television set, enthralled by the drama that was unfolding before her eyes. She watched as Xie Huilin opened the shoot-out with a goal for China, was transfixed when Carla Overbeck scored to tie the game, 1–1.

Another shot for China, another goal.

Another shot for the US, another goal, this one by Joy Fawcett, a defensive player who had played every minute of the tournament for the US

Briana Scurry, the goalkeeper for Team USA, stopped Liu Ying on China's next shot. The US took the lead when Kristine Lilly scored on her third-round attempt.

The two teams traded goals in the fourth round; then Sun Wen scored on China's fifth shot. Both teams had scored four goals by the time Brandi Chastain strode forward and purposefully placed the ball on the white circle in the middle of the field, twelve yards in front of the goal.

Becky could barely breathe. Few of the forty million people watching on TV probably could. She was glued to the screen as Chastain set up for the shot. In case anyone had forgotten, the announcer on ABC reminded everyone that four months earlier, in the final of the Algarve Cup, Chastain had missed a penalty kick, and the United States lost that game to China, by one goal.

Chastain made her approach. Then the right-footed kicker blasted a shot with her left foot that found its way into the right side of China's goal. She immediately ripped off her game jersey (a move popular with many men playing at that time) and, in her black sports bra, dropped to her knees, fists clenched in celebration, providing the moment many fans will never forget. It was the image captured on the covers of *Sports Illustrated* and *Newsweek*.

But it's not what Becky remembers most.

She jumped to her feet and watched as the tide of white jerseys swept onto the field and swallowed up Brandi Chastain. Becky had witnessed a level of elation she had never seen before, never even knew existed. Even as a teenage spectator 1,800 miles away, it was a moment that would change her life.

"That game was so big for me," Becky said. "The

look of joy on their faces knowing they had won. It was such a close match, so competitive, such a high level of play, so many people watching. They were just so happy. I knew right then that I needed to feel what they were feeling, that I wanted to know what it felt to win something that big."

In the aftermath of perhaps the most exciting moment in the history of women's sports in America, Becky had found herself a new goal.

And unlike pretty much everyone else who has ever seen such a moment and dreamed what it might be like to live something like it, Becky actually got to experience it for herself. More than once.

She felt it first on the podium after winning the 2012 Olympics. Officials from the Games were about to hand out the gold medals when it dawned on Becky that she was having a once-in-a-lifetime feeling. But she was wrong.

She had it again, three years later, after winning the 2015 Women's World Cup. She found herself running around the field inside BC Place, the arena in Vancouver, British Columbia, Canada, where the US had just defeated Japan, 5–2, to win the World Cup. Her parents were up in the stands, just as they always were, watching their daughter do what she loved most in the world. Her brothers were there, too, cheering on their little sister; she'd come a long way from those roller-hockey games on the street in front of their house. Tim and Jennifer Boul, her J. B. Marine former coaches, were there, watching with Becky's family (a far more exotic trip than that first one to Peoria so many years earlier). Her college coach—one of the coaches responsible for her making that first U-16 national team—was there, on the sidelines, sharing in this glorious accomplishment.

Becky was soaking it all up. She and Meghan Klingenberg—her teammate and partner on defense and one of her closest friends—carried an American flag together as they circled the stadium in celebration.

"I was thinking, 'Can you believe this? We did it!'" Becky said, smiling at the memory.

The world of women's soccer changed in the US in the wake of that World Cup, just as there had been a dramatic uptick in participation after that summer of 1999. More kids were playing in rec leagues across the country, more schools were adding girls' soccer to their athletic departments.

The Sauerbrunns certainly noticed it. St. Louis had always been a soccer town, but suddenly people who had never paid attention to women's soccer in their lives were coming up to Jane and Scott to talk about what Becky and her team had done.

Tim Boul noticed it, too. Once, he was working his way through the aisles of a local grocery store, wearing his Team USA replica sweatshirt, the one emblazoned with Becky's name and the number 4. An older gentleman, maybe eighty years old, spotted the sweatshirt and stopped Tim to talk.

"Are you Becky Sauerbrunn's father?" he asked.

"No," Tim said. "I coached her back in club ball."

Tim was giggling to himself over the attention he was getting thanks to Becky's accomplishments, when he heard a voice behind him. Another man had heard the exchange, and as Tim turned toward him he heard, "Hey! Good job not screwing her up."

What is most special to Becky is when she sees the young girls who have taken up the game. So many of them play soccer now, it's rare when there aren't enough girls to field a team and a girl has to find a spot on a boys' team just to have the chance to play.

"Seeing these young girls playing makes me so happy," Becky said. "These girls don't have any idea where the ceiling might be for them."

Becky loves the opportunities she has to interact with the youngest generation of soccer-playing girls. She remembers how cool it was when she first had the chance to meet Brandi Chastain in person, how excited she was—and she was already a member of the U-19s by that time. So every chance she gets, Becky stops to talk with the girls, to answer their questions and sign autographs for them if they ask. She's nearly missed many a team bus leaving a game or a training facility, because she's been making sure she signs for and speaks to every last child waiting for her.

Her commitment to the future of the sport, though, goes beyond autographs and answering questions. Becky and several teammates decided to tackle the issue of inequality, hoping to be able to resolve it before future generations of girls ever have to face it.

In late March 2016, five members of the US Women's National Team—Carli Lloyd, Hope Solo, Alex Morgan, Megan Rapinoe, and Becky—filed a complaint with the Equal Employment Opportunity Commission, claiming that their team's play-

Becky Sauerbrunn ✓
@beckysauerbrunn

👤 Follow ⌄

Five players signed the complaint, but the decision to file was whole-heartedly supported by the entire team. #equalplayequalpay #thegals

RETWEETS	LIKES
1,772	4,841

6:07 AM - 31 Mar 2016

↩ 103   🔁 1.8K   🤍 4.8K

ers are paid significantly less to do their jobs than their counterparts on the men's National Team. Becky announced the initiative that morning to her thousands of followers on Twitter.

Wage inequality in the workplace is not an issue exclusive to soccer. Women have been waging a fight for fairness in the workplace for decades, and the issue of equal pay elbowed its way into the conversation for many candidates running for president during their 2016 primary and general election campaigns. Hours after the news broke that a complaint had been filed, Hillary Clinton responded with a tweet of her own, noting, "Every woman deserves equal pay." It's a societal issue that affects women across all industries at all levels. And the members of the US Women's National Team wanted to do their part to bring attention to this important problem.

"The scope of this fight goes beyond women's soccer," Becky said. "Every day, I question why there is even an argument anymore. Why do people fight so hard against this principle? Why is it so threatening to so many people?"

The US Women's National Team players had a strong point they wanted to make clear. They were contractually obligated to play a minimum of twenty "friendlies" a year—exhibition games, or matches played in preparation for an upcoming tournament. They would be paid a certain amount for winning each friendly and a lesser amount if they lost.

Sounds fair, right? It does until you hear their argument that the US men's team gets paid the same rate, win or lose. And that they got paid considerably more than the women's team.

The women didn't bring this case to point out how much more successful their program has been than the men's (though that point is inarguable and undeniable). They brought the case to show that men and women were being paid at different rates by the same employer—the US Soccer Federation—for doing the same job, regardless of the fact that revenues (money generated by the programs through things like television contracts, jersey sales, and tickets to games) actually show that the women's team makes more money than the men.

Make no mistake: Women's soccer established itself in 2015 as a major player on the American sports scene. When actor Tom Hanks is cheering you on in his social media accounts, stirring his thirteen million Twitter followers to support you, you're officially big-time. (In one tweet, Hanks singled out Becky, saying "Thank you, Becks!" presumably for her role in leading the National Team to the knockout round of the 2015 Women's World Cup.)

Twenty-three million people watched that World Cup final. Only seventeen million watched the men's World Cup final the summer before (granted, the audience would have been much larger had the US men been in the final—which they never have been). Game 7 of the 2014 World Series drew only a slightly larger TV audience than the Women's World Cup, and ratings for Game 6 of the 2015 NBA Finals were virtually identical.

Becky and her teammates gratefully acknowledge the opportunities created for them by the members of the '99ers—Brandi Chastain, Mia Hamm, and Julie Foudy. In the fifteen years following that monumental moment at the Rose Bowl, participation in girls' soccer at the high-school level grew by more than 45 percent (according to the National Federation of State High School Associations). Volleyball was up nearly 13 percent; fast-pitch softball was up about 7 percent.

Girls' soccer is growing, and leaders of the National Team felt it was their obligation to take the lead on the issue of equal pay for equal play.

"Ask any athlete what their ultimate goal is, and that would be to leave their sport better than they found it," Becky said. "It goes beyond winning a gold medal or playing for a world championship. I am so proud to be a part of this group of women who are bringing this issue to light. It is a legacy that any member of our team would be proud to leave behind."

The women of the National Team take seriously their relationship with the next generation of girls' soccer players and women's soccer fans. They always have, dating back well before they took their fight for equality public. Just before leaving for Canada and the 2015 World Cup, the US

Women's National Team launched its #SheBelieves campaign. They posted an open letter, signed by everyone on the team, on the US Soccer website, addressed to young girls everywhere:

You, with your cleats on and a ball at your feet.

You, with your nose in a book and a dream in your head.

You, with your hand in the air, asking question after question after question.

Listen up, ladies: we believe in you.

We believe in your dreams, in your goals, and in your ability to reach them. It might be an uphill battle, and you will get knocked down, but it's your battle. Own it. Fight it. Never give up on it.

You got this!

As a team, your team, we feel your energy. We read your tweets, see your photos on Instagram, follow as you share your brilliant minds, and hear when you cheer from the stands.

We believe we will be at the top of the podium after that final whistle blows. We never let anyone tell us otherwise. Don't let the tired clichés and stereotypes make you doubt what you are meant to be: the best.

You support us and show us the way. Now it's time to turn it around and let you know we have your back. We are going to give everything to reach our goals and we want you to do that, too.

We want you to believe you can be the best: the best athlete, the best student, the best doctor, lawyer, teacher, writer. We want you to be the best you.

Share your dream with us using the hashtag #SheBelieves. Tweet us, post it on Facebook and send us photos on Instagram to show us how you are working towards this dream.

We believe in you.

#SheBelieves

The responsibility to pay it forward continues to drive Becky Sauerbrunn. Soccer to her is one big, welcoming, growing community. Now it's her turn to make sure today's players are afforded the same opportunities that benefited her.

"I take a lot of pride in making sure those girls know how much we appreciate what they're doing," Becky said. "We were them at one point."

Don't expect that Becky's final contribution to the sport she loves will be made in a courtroom. More than likely, it will be made out on the field, where her focus remains, as always, to become a better player tomorrow than she is today.

Even in the final few months spent preparing for the 2016 Summer Olympics in Brazil—and then after the Rio Games, during which Team USA shockingly was eliminated by Sweden in the quarter-final round—Becky knew there remained room for her to grow and improve. She'd seen glimpses of how good she believes she can be (she was, after all, a finalist for the 2016 US Soccer Female Player of the Year award). She knew she was not there yet. But she knows what it takes to get there.

"None of us would have made it without people who supported us and believed in us," Becky said. "That's the message: self-belief. Who knows where that belief can take you?"

ACKNOWLEDGMENTS

Gathering stories and experiences from Becky Sauerbrunn's childhood and soccer career would not have been possible without her willing participation in this project. I am grateful to Becky for her generosity with her time, for her candor, and for her cooperation. I also want to thank Becky's family, who shared their time and memories with me—her parents, Jane and Scott, and her brothers, Grant and Adam. Thank you to two of her longtime coaches, who took the time to talk about one of their favorite subjects: Tim Boul of J. B. Marine and Steve Swanson. Their time with Becky ranged from the ODP national team to the

University of Virginia and all the way up to the US Women's National Team. I thank Aaron Heifetz, the US Women's National Team press officer for US Soccer, who helped get the ball rolling on this story.

Finally, many thanks go out to Rick Richter at Aevitas Creative Management and to Fiona Simpson and Mara Anastas and their talented team at Simon & Schuster for their belief in and support for the Real Sports series from the start.

ABOUT THE AUTHOR

David Seigerman's love of sports was kindled on the ball fields of his Long Island childhood, then fanned while rooting for the Mets, Jets, and Rangers through some historically bad seasons in the 1970s and 1980s. Upon realizing that his best path to the big leagues would be not with a bat but with a pen, he graduated from Ithaca College a million years ago and began a career as a sports journalist. He has been thrilled by the privilege of covering games and telling stories about athletes across all levels of all sports—including that 1999 Women's World Cup team that captivated a young Becky Sauerbrunn's attention (specifically, its 3–0 tournament-opening win over Denmark at Giants Stadium and the 3–2 quarterfinal victory over Germany in Landover, Maryland)—for pretty much every storytelling medium there is: newspapers, magazines, television, radio, digital, documentaries, and books. Prior to the Real Sports series, David coauthored several books, including *Take Your Eye Off the Ball: How to Watch Football by Knowing Where to Look* and *Quarterback: The Toughest Job in Pro Sports* (both with Pat Kirwan), and *Under Pressure: How Playing Football Almost Cost Me Everything and Why I'd Do It All Again* (with Ray Lucas). Aside from a goal scored in a beginners' men's ice-hockey league (February 7, 2013) and an honest-to-goodness hole in one (June 5, 2015—with witnesses), his most treasured sports moments have come from coaching and watching his daughter and son on the ball fields and skating rinks of their own Westchester County childhoods.

ABOUT REAL CONTENT MEDIA GROUP

Real Content Media Group creates, produces, and distributes content across all forms of media, including television, radio, Internet, OTT digital networks, social media, syndication, and publishing. We specialize in the seamless integration of content and products to form salable media brands that speak very clearly to targeted audiences. Using our strategic network, we currently distribute content, products, and services in the Sports and Health & Wellness verticals.

DEC 2 1 2017